For My Daughter

_____

From

_____

Dreams for My Daughter

Illustrated by Becky Kelly

Written by Polly Blair

**Andrews McMeel
Publishing, LLC**

Kansas City

06 07 08 09 10 EPB 10 9 8 7 6 5 4 3 2 1

ISBN-13: 978-0-7407-6174-4
ISBN-10: 0-7407-6174-9

www.andrewsmcmeel.com
www.beckykelly.com

Illustrations by Becky Kelly
Design by Stephanie R. Farley
Edited by Polly Blair & Jean Lucas
Production by Elizabeth Nuelle

Dreams for My Daughter

Every day you surprise me,
impress and inspire me.

I loved you before I even
saw your face.

I dreamed of the fun
we'd have together

and of the tea parties we would host.

My daughter, while I can't be with you
every step of the way,

my arms and heart are always open for you,
and I wish for you these gifts:

An ocean-wide sense of wonder

and an open heart for love.

I wish for you the joy of
catching snowflakes on your tongue,

B. Kelly

playing with best friends,

getting lost in a good book,

and time to dream.

I wish you remember to test the water first,
but know sometimes you will just need to jump in!

I wish for you the joy of giving, and forgiving,
and of giving thanks.

I wish for you to know that
you will find rainbows
even on umbrella days.

I wish for you the gift of knowing
that mistakes are part of growing.

Hurts will heal, because you'll find
that laughter is truly the best medicine.

I treasure every time we giggle together,
cry together, and smile together.

My daughter, you are my bright star.
You sparkle and glitter and shine.

I wish for every day to be a wonderful adventure.

There is nothing you can't do.
I believe in you.